First Facts®

American Indian Homes
WICKIUPS

by Riley Flynn

CAPSTONE PRESS
a capstone imprint

First Facts are published by Capstone Press,
1710 Roe Crest Drive, North Mankato, Minnesota 56003
www.capstonepub.com

Library of Congress Cataloging-in-Publication Data
Flynn, Riley.
  Wickiups / by Riley Flynn.
    pages cm. — (First facts. American Indian homes)
  Summary: "Informative, engaging text and vivid photos introduce readers to American Indian wickiups"—Provided by publisher.
  Includes bibliographical references and index.
  ISBN 978-1-4914-2056-0 (library binding)
  ISBN 978-1-4914-2242-7 (paperback)
  ISBN 978-1-4914-2262-5 (eBook PDF)
1. Indians of North America—Dwellings—Great Basin—Juvenile literature. 2. Wickiups—Great Basin—Juvenile literature. I. Title.
  E78.G67F55 2015   392.3'608997—dc23

                                                    2014025810

Editorial Credits

Anna Butzer, editor; Sarah Bennett, designer; Tracy Cummins, media researcher;
Gene Bentdahl, production specialist

Photo Credits

Alamy: Marek Zuk, 21, Tom Bean, 17; Capstone Press: 6; The Denver Public Library: Western History Collection/X-33387, 11; Library of Congress: 5, 9; Nativestock: Marilyn Angel Wynn, 15, 19; Newscom: akg-images, 13; Photoshot: Nativestock, Front Cover, UPPA/Marilyn Angel Wynn, 1; Shutterstock: SARIN KUNTHONG, Back Cover, Design Element; Wikimedia: NARA, 7.

Printed in the United States of America in North Mankato, Minnesota.
092014   008482CGS15

Table of Contents

What Is a Wickiup?

Wickiups are simple dome-shaped shelters. American Indians built wickiups out of wood, brush, and grass.

Wickiups varied in size. People often built wickiups about 8 feet (2.4 meters) high and 10 to 15 feet (3 to 5 m) wide.

Who Lived in Wickiups?

Some tribes found in what is now the western United States lived in wickiups. The Paiute, Shoshone, and Ute lived in a large desert region called the Great Basin. They lived off the land hunting and gathering food. These **tribes** moved in small groups called **bands**.

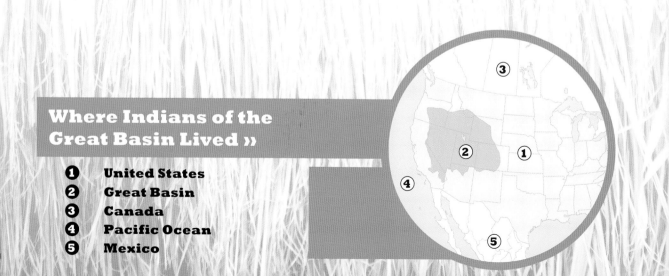

Where Indians of the Great Basin Lived »

1. United States
2. Great Basin
3. Canada
4. Pacific Ocean
5. Mexico

The Apache Indians were also known to use wickiups. They lived in the Southwest desert region of the United States.

tribe—a group of people who share the same ancestors, customs, and laws

band—a group of related people who live and hunt together

Chapter 3

Gathering Materials

The Indians of the Great Basin region used a variety of materials to build wickiups. Builders looked for willow or oak **saplings**. They cut the wood to make poles for the **frame** of a wickiup.

People gathered grass and brush to cover the outside of the wickiup. They twisted **reeds** or strips of bark together to make twine.

A man stands outside a wickiup in 1901.

FACT

Builders lined some wickiups with bark to keep the houses warm during colder months.

sapling—a young tree

frame—the basic shape over which a house is built

reeds—tall grass with long, narrow leaves and joined stems

Chapter 4

Preparing the Site

Women often built the wickiups. First they found an area with dry, flat ground. They drew a circle to mark where they would build the wickiup. Then the materials that were gathered were brought to the **site**.

FACT

Men hunted for food instead of building shelters. They fed and protected their families.

site—the position or location of something

Chapter 5

Building a Wickiup

Making the frame was the first step in building a wickiup. Builders pushed thin poles in the ground and bent them inward to make a dome shape. They tied the poles together at the top with twine. They then covered the frame with grass, brush, or branches. Builders left an opening at the front of the wickiup for a doorway.

FACT

American Indians dug a small fire pit into the center of a wickiup. A fire kept the inside of the wickiup warm during cold weather.

Chapter 6

Inside a Wickiup

Wickiups were very dark inside. The only openings on a wickiup were the smoke hole and doorway.

People did not spend much time inside wickiups. They cooked and did other daily tasks outside. They mainly used wickiups for shelter at night while they slept.

FACT

The curved surface of wickiups made them great shelters in many different weather conditions. The dome shape allowed wind to pass around the home instead of knocking it down.

surface—the outside or outermost area of something

15

Chapter 7

Wickiup Villages

When bands found a hunting spot they built a temporary village. Builders could put up several wickiups quickly. When they couldn't find any more food people moved to a new area.

People built their wickiups in different sizes. Many were large enough to hold a family. Some were large enough to hold only one hunter.

FACT
When American Indian families moved they left the wickiups behind.

Chapter 8

Ramadas

The Great Basin Indians spent a lot of time outdoors. To protect themselves from the sun they built a roofed shelter called a ramada. It had a brush roof supported by four poles. People sat under a ramada during the day. It was used as a place to rest and visit.

Pieces of History

American Indians no longer need to use wickiups. But people still build wickiups to share the history of the tribes that once used them.

Amazing but True

American Indians who built wickiups did not take time to build furniture. All they really needed was a place to sleep. They gathered bark from juniper trees to use as beds inside their wickiups. With no furniture tribes could move quickly.

Glossary

band (BAND)—many small family groups joined together

frame (FRAYM)—the basic shape over which a house is built

reeds (REEDS)—tall grass with long, narrow leaves and joined stems

sapling (SAP-ling)—a young tree

site (SITE)—the position or location of something

surface (SUR-fiss)—the outside or outermost area of something

tribe (TRIBE)—a group of people who share the same ancestors, customs, and laws

Read More

McDaniel, Melissa. *Great Basin Indians.* First Nations of North America. Chicago: Heinemann Library, 2012.

Jensen-Elliot, Cindy. *Desert Communities Past and Present.* Who Lived Here?. North Mankato, Minn.: Capstone Press, 2014.

Internet Sites

FactHound offers a safe, fun way to find Internet sites related to this book. All of the sites on FactHound have been researched by our staff.

Here's all you do:

Visit *www.facthound.com*

Type in this code: 9781491420560

 Check out projects, games and lots more at
www.capstonekids.com

Critical Thinking Using the Common Core

1. What is a ramada? How was it used? (Key Ideas and Details)

2. Look at the Fact box on page 13. What is the author trying to say? Did American Indians keep the wickiups warm in other ways? If so, how? (Integration of Knowledge and Ideas)

Index